The

MW00720789

Rants, Raves

THOUGHTS

of

MOAMMER KHADAFY

HE DICTATOR IN HIS OWN WORDS + THOSE OF OTHERS

OYO

{Moammer Al–Khadafy}

Publisher
Jeff Brauer

Editor
Julian Smith

Art
Eric Chun

ON YOUR OWN PUBLICATIONS, LLC
Corporate Address:
Brooklyn Navy Yard
Building 120, Suite 207
Brooklyn, NY 11205

Tel: 718.875.9455
Fax: 561.673.2436
Email: oyobooks@yahoo.com

ISBN 1-929377-17-7

Thanks for checking out OYO's Rants, Raves and Thoughts series. The goals of and inspiration for these books are:

1. To explain what makes dictators and terrorists so ruthless, in their own words, in the words of others, and through jokes created by people who lived under their rule and influence.

2. To demonstrate what a talented group of free-thinking writers and graphic designers can do with access to a database of information and a limitless imagination about how to let the words of these powerful, psychotic people reveal who they are, what they believe and what they hope to achieve.

3. To give closure to 15 years of personal exploration that started with a trip through China that coincided with the massacre in Tiananmen Square and ended with the terrorist attacks on my beloved home (New York City) and birthplace (Washington DC). Long live freedom and the right to say, learn, write and publish what you want!

Jeff Brauer, *Publisher*

TABLE OF CONTENTS

Moammer Al-Khadafy was born the youngest child of a nomadic family of Bedouins near Sirte, Libya in 1942. He spent his early years learning to hate the West: his grandfather had been killed by an Italian colonist in 1911, and he grew up hearing of the exploitation of his people by "the foreigners."

An outstanding student, Khadafy soon turned his attention to revolutionary politics, inspired by Egyptian statesman Gamal Abdul Nasser's appeals for Arab unity. After attending military academy in Britain in 1966, he returned to join with fellow militants to plot the overthrow of the pro-Western monarchy of King Idris Senussi I in 1969.

Khadafy has remained firmly in power since then, surviving many assassination attempts from within and outside his own government. His use of Libya's oil wealth to support revolutionary and terrorist groups worldwide has earned worldwide condemnation and severed diplomatic ties.

Libya's ties to terrorism led to U.S. bombing raids on Tripoli in April 1985 which injured Khadafy, killed his 15-month-old adopted daughter, and wounded two of his sons, ages 3 and 4. International sanctions followed Khadafy's refusal to hand over two Libya suspects in the bombing of Pan Am flight 103 plane over Lockerbie, Scotland in 1988. The two were eventually handed over, but U.S. sanctions remain in place.

Khadafy's plans to unite Libya, Egypt, and Syria into a pan-Arab state have come to naught, while the results of his cultural and social changes at home have been mixed. The political and personal philosophy described in his Green Book combines elements of Arab nationalism, Islamic fundamentalism, the welfare state, and a personal brand of popular democracy.

Khadafy's flamboyant personal style includes a taste for designer clothes and a phalanx of heavily armed female bodyguards, said to remain virgins during their service. His hatred of the West is matched only by his volatile temper and unpredictable behavior.

POLITI-
CAL
THE-
ORY

"I wish Afghanistan had become Communist; the situation in the world would have been much better than it is now."

– Interview, *Libyan Television Network, August 29, 1997*

"Political struggle that results in the victory of a candidate with 51 percent of the votes leads to a dictorial governing body disguised as a false democracy, since 49 percent of the electorate is ruled by an instrument of governing they did not vote for, but had imposed upon them. This is

Dictatorship."

– The Green Book, *Part 1, Chapter 1*

"My all-out objective and goal

is to instigate and inspire the masses and the people to govern themselves and to reach authority. What is taking place in the world is just the opposite. The rulers are using power against the people to reach authority."

– Interview, *December 1997*

"Nationalism in the world of man and group instinct in the animal kingdom are like gravity in the domain of mineral and celestial bodies. If the mass of the sun were smashed so that it lost its gravity, the gases would blow away and its unity would no longer exist."

– The Green Book, *Part 3, Chapter 1*

"Under genuine democracy there is

no excuse for

one class to crush other classes

for its own benefit,

no excuse for

one party to crush other parties

for its own interests,

no excuse for

one tribe to crush other tribes

for its own benefit

and no excuse for

one sect to crush other sects

for its own interests."

–The Green Book, *Part 1, Chapter 4*

"What is said about [Islamic] fundamentalism is not right. Fundamentalism is not violence and is not terrorism. We are the advocates of fundamentalism and those who nurture it. We are the ones who revived it and the Libyan revolution is considered as responsible for the revival of fundamentalism and awakening in the Islamic world."
–Interview, *Libyan Television Network, August 29, 1997*

"The purpose of the new Socialist society

is to create a society which is happy because it is free. This can be achieved through satisfying the material and spiritual needs of man, and that, in turn, comes about through the liberation of these needs from outside domination and control."

– The Green Book, *Part 2, Chapter 2*

"The Third Universal Theory [described in The Green Book] is a herald to the masses announcing the final salvation from all fetters of injustice, despotism, exploitation and economic and political hegemony. It has the purpose of establishing the society of all people, where all men are free and equal in authority, wealth and arms, so that freedom may gain the final and complete triumph."

– The Green Book, *Part 2, Chapter 4*

"Finally, the era of the masses, which follows the age of the republics, excites the feelings and dazzles the eyes...The Third Universal Theory heralds emancipation from the fetters of injustice, despotism, exploitation and economic and political hegemony, for the purpose of establishing a society of all the people where all are free and have equal share in authority, wealth and arms. Freedom will then triumph definitively and universally."

– The Green Book, *Part 1, Chapter 10*

"The Green Book announces to the people the happy discovery of the way to direct democracy, in a practical form…All that the masses need do now is to struggle to put an end to all forms of dictatorial rule in the world today, to all forms of what is falsely called democracy."

– The Green Book, *Part 1, Chapter 6*

"The final step is when the new Socialist society reaches the stage where profit and money disappear…through reaching, in production, the level where the material needs of the members of society are satisfied. In that final stage profit will automatically disappear and there will be no need for money."

– The Green Book, *Part 2, Chapter 3*

"The social bond which binds together each human group, from the family through the tribe to the nation, is the basis for the movement of history…It is the nature of life itself. Other animals, apart from man, live in groups. Indeed, the group is the basis for the survival of all groups within the animal kingdom. So nationalism is the basis for the survival of nations."

– The Green Book, *Part 3, Chapter 1*

PHI-
LOSOP
HY

“If they attack me, I’ll become a madman.”

–Speaking to Western diplomat on the consequence of an attack on Libya by the U.S. or Israel, *Chicago Tribune, January 10, 1986*

"If a group of people wear white clothes in mourning and another group puts on black ones, the sentiment of each group will be adjusted according to these two colors, i.e. one group hates the black color while the other one likes it, and vice versa. Such a sentiment leaves its physical effect on the cells as well as on the genes in the body."

– The Green Book, *Part 3, Chapter 9*

“The natural person has freedom to express himself even if, when he is mad, he behaves irrationally to express his madness.”

– The Green Book, Part 1, *Chapter 10*

"Different types of boxing and wrestling are evidence that mankind has not got rid of all savage behavior. Inevitably they will come to an end when man ascends the ladder of civilization."

– The Green Book, *Part 3, Chapter 10*

"Truly, the earth is your mother; she gave birth to you from her insides. She is the one who nursed you and fed you. Do not be disobedient to your mother—and do not shear her hair, cut off her limbs, rip her flesh, or wound her body. You must only trim her nails, make her body clean of dirt or filth. Give her medicine to cure any disease. Do not place great weights above her breast, weights of mud or stone above her ribs. Respect her, and remember that if you are too harsh with her, you will not find another."

Escape to Hell and Other Stories (1998)

Khadafy is visiting a school in Tripoli. In one class, he asks the students if anyone can give him an example of a "tragedy."

One little boy stands up and says, "If my best friend who lives next door was playing in the street when a car came along and killed him, that would be a tragedy."

"No," Khadafy says, "That would be an accident."

A girl raises her hand. "If a school bus carrying fifty Iraqi children drove off a cliff, killing everyone involved...that would be a tragedy."

"I'm afraid not," explains Khadafy. "That is what we would call a great loss."

None of the other children volunteered. "What?" asks Khadafy, "Isn't there any one here who can give me an example of a tragedy?"

Finally, a boy in the back raises his hand. In a

timid voice, he speaks: "If an airplane carrying Yasser Arafat, Saddam Hussein, and Colonel Khadafy were blown up by a bomb, that would be a tragedy."

"Wonderful!" Khadafy beams. "Marvelous! And can you tell me why that would be a tragedy?"

"Well," says the boy, "because it wouldn't be an accident, and it certainly would be no great loss!"

"Life in the city is merely a wormlike biological existence where man lives and dies meaninglessly"

– Escape to Hell and Other Stories (1998)

"Those who are unable to perform the roles of heroism in life, who are ignorant of the events of history, who fall short of envisaging the future and who are not serious enough in their lives, are the trivial persons who fill the seats of the theatres and cinemas to watch the events of life and to learn their course. They are like pupils who occupy school desks because they are not only uneducated but also illiterate. Those who direct the course of life for themselves do not need to watch it working through actors on the stage or in the cinemas."

– The Green Book, *Part 3, Chapter 10*

"Horsemen who hold the reins of their horses have no seat in the grandstands at the race-course. If every person has a horse, no one will be there to watch and applaud. The sitting spectators are only those who are too helpless to perform this kind of activity because they are not horsemen."

– The Green Book, Part 3, Chapter 10

The Green Book, *Part 2, Chapter 1*

"He who produces is the one who consumes."

"It is impossible

– On the Western perception of Islamic fundamentalism extremists,
interview, Libyan Television Network, August 29, 1997

for a Muslim to kill children and women and burn them, as the case in Algeria, or to kill a poor policeman in southern Egypt who is working for a living to bring up his children."

"Mankind

is really still backward because man does not speak with his brother one common language which is inherited and not learned. However, it is only a matter of time for mankind to achieve that goal unless civilization should relapse."

–The Green Book, *Part 3, Chapter 9*

"All of history's conflicts throughout the ages have been led by

man against man,

or against nature, have been about land. Land has been the crux of the conflict."

–Escape to Hell and Other Stories (1998)

"Compulsory education, of which countries of the world boast whenever they are able to force it on their youth, is one of the methods which suppresses freedom. It is a compulsory obliteration of a human being's talents as well as a forcible direction of a human being's choices."

"Compulsory education, of which countries of the world boast whenever they are able to force it on their youth, is one of the methods which suppresses freedom. It is a compulsory obliteration of a human being's talents as well as a forcible direction of a human being's choices."

– The Green Book, *Part 3, Chapter 8*

"Domestic servants, paid or unpaid, are a type of slave. Indeed they are the slaves of the modern age."

– The Green Book, *Part 2, Chapter 4*

"Man's freedom is lacking if somebody else controls what he needs. For need may result in man's enslavement of man. Need causes exploitation."

– The Green Book, *Part 2, Chapter 2*

THE RACES

"The Arabs and the Blacks are very much kindred and related together, moı than any other peoples. In Asia, we don't have Blacks. In Europe, we don have Blacks either. In America, they know Blacks as slaves brought fror Africa to work there. But the Africans and the Arabs live together on one teı ritory, on one land."

– Interview, *December 1997*

"We are committed to give our support and confidence to the Nation of Islam in America led by my dear brother and friend, Mr. Louis Farrakhan. This help and assistance is not expressed and manifested in numbers, because it is not an account in a bank and it is not a kind of a loan. We give support and confidence that is unlimited and unwavering and it is the responsibility or the problem of those who want to translate this kind of aid and assistance into numerical figures."

– Interview, *December 1997*

"We are committed to give our support and confidence to the

"We

–Referring to his offer of $1 million to Louis Farrakan's Nation of Islam for human rights work, which the U.S. government prohibited the group from collecting, *Libyan Television Network, August 29, 1997*

Nation of Islam in America led by my dear brother and friend."

– Interview with Askia Muhammad,
Washington Bureau Chief, Nation of Islam

do not care if their feelings were provoked. Let their nerves get racked, God willing, what we are interested in is justice."

"The black race is now in a very backward social situation. But such backwardness helps to bring about numerical superiority of the blacks because their low standard of living has protected them from getting to know the means and ways of birth control and family planning. Also their backward social traditions are a reason why there is no limit to marriage, leading to their unlimited growth, while the population of other races has decreased because of birth control, restrictions on marriage and continuous occupation in work, unlike the blacks who are sluggish in a climate which is always hot."

– The Green Book, *Part 3, Chapter 7*

"This imperialist country must be

destroyed

Otherwise the nation of blacks will be

destroyed,

Islam will be

destroyed,

the state of Red Indians will be

destroyed.

We are ready to give you arms because your cause is just.
We are with you, don't worry. You have to trust us...
The final victory will be soon."

–Speaking by satellite to Black Muslim convention in Chicago, *The Washington Post, February 25, 1985*

ISRAEL\ PALES- TINE

“[The Israelis] want to destroy all other nations...until there is only them, the chosen people of God. We don’t want the Soviet Union, or America, or the Asians. Let us fight, even with knives, but let them leave us alone to fight as we want.”

–Interview, calling on outsiders to let Israelis and Arabs settle differences themselves, *The Associated Press, January 13, 1986*

"Unless Palestine is

liberated, the centers

of terrorism, America

and Israel, should

– United Press International, *January 1, 1986*

be eradicated."

"As an independent state we do not condone such acts. But as for the Palestinians—it may well be necessary for them. Libya will not hesitate to provide what the Palestinian resistance demands for the liberation of Palestine."

–Speaking on terrorism, *The Washington Post, January 10, 1986*

"We support [the Palestinians'] just cause but Libya cannot be responsible for their tactics. We tell them to liberate their homeland, but [if they attack] I cannot call them back."

–United Press International, *May 5, 1986*

WAR

“American Soldiers . . .

must be turned into lambs and eating them is tolerated.”

– Two months after U.S. bombing raid on Tripoli, *June 15, 1986*

"We can swim in the sea with mines strapped to our bodies... We will change ourselves into mined whales in the Mediterranean if we decide to die and the United States will never be able to destroy an entire people."

–The Associated Press, *January 16, 1986*

"If it comes to war,

we will drag Europe into it...

We [will] have to close our eyes and ears and

hit indiscriminately...

We [will] react with suicide,

squads against towns, ports, wherever the

threats are—while at the same time the

Americans are far away."

–Warning of the consequences of an attack on Libya by the U.S. from European bases, *The Washington Post, January 10, 1986*

"All **military** aircraft or cruise missiles must be placed inside museums. The best solution is to address the economic, political and medical bases [of international disputes]."

–Jamahiriya News Agency, *October 20, 2001*

"International responsibility and reason require that all aircraft and all guns should fall silent, to listen to the voice of reason and to solve the problems of nations... We have to acquire moral courage, not military courage... All human hostilities or animosities have to end and disappear."

–Jamahiriya News Agency, *October 20, 2001*

AMER-
ICA

"If the Americans land on the Libyan coast… they will burn, they will die… and the [Lybian coastal cities] will become the slaughterhouses for the sheep of America."

– Speech, Libyan television, *May 9, 19*

"We are capable of
destroying America
and breaking
its nose."

—Address two months after U.S.
bombing raid on Tripoli, *June 15, 1986*

"America is dominating the world and doing whatever it wishes with it."

–Interview, *Libyan Television Network, August 29, 1997*

"We want to see America's pressure America bombed us with nuclear bombs. To hell with America."

–Interview, *Libyan Television Network, August 29, 1997*

After the bombing of the Federal building in Oklahoma City, Khadafy claimed that the bombing signaled the start of a mass revolt against the U.S. government—"a reaction against the nightmare and tyranny"—and offered Clinton refuge in Libya as "the only safe country in the world."

–The Washington Times, *May 1, 1995*

An April Fool's Day joke.

–Describing the invitation extended to Israeli Labor Party Secretary–General Ra'anan Cohen by Libyan congress member Miloud Chaabane Gammoudi, *The Review, May 2000*

The one who is making an April fool of himself is Khadafy.

–Response of Cohen's spokesman Yerah Tal to Khadafy's rebuff, *The Review, May 2000*

Sheik Zubayr bin William was Shakespeare. Shake came from Sheik.

–Joke told to Tunisian parliament, December 1988, while recounting how Arabs had taught Europeans medicine, geography, time–keeping, astronomy and literature, *The Daily Telegraph, August 4, 1989*

"You take the world so lightly. You don't see any respectable press, but to suggest to us an American Air Force base? I will call this bully-ism. This is a bully-boy attitude used by the Americans. It is quite clear that we go to an Air Force base and they are going to hijack them from that Air Force base."

–On U.S. requests to hand over suspects in Lockerbie bombing trial, *Federal News Service, October 10, 1998* will have to pay the price: [the lives of] American citizens."

–Newsweek, *February 22, 1988*

"The Americans have been misled, because Zionism owns the mass media. It gives the American people the wrong idea about Khadafy, about Islam, and about the outside world."

—*The Associated Press*, January 9, 1986

"I don't believe that the American people have any influence in affecting the American policy because the system in America is a dictatorship... [The American people] only know the world through the American newspapers. These newspapers are ruled and governed by hostile, racist circles... For this reason the American people don't know the truth. If you ask them, "How do you know Khadafy? How did you come to know Khadafy?" They will answer, that they knew from CNN or The Washington Post."

–Interview, *December 1997*

"The radios of America, states and Israel are the intention of destroying Islam means killing chil- Algeria now: murdering their bodies and blind without aim or program say] the Libyan revolu- America and colonial- dom and unity, so go against it."

Britain, the Western ones that say…with the Islam, "See, this is Islam, dren, as is happening in women and burning killing and revenge or distinction. [They tion stands against ism by the side of free- and declare [war]

–Interview, *Libyan Television Network, August 29, 1997*

U.S.
PRESI-
DENTS

"Flaky"

"A pariah"

"An unstable

–Terms used by President Ronald Reagan to describe Khadafy

barbarian"

"The mad dog of

the Middle East"

"Hitler #2"

"Israeli dog"

"A useless actor"

–Names Khadafy has called Ronald Reagan, while referring to the U.S.

"Crazy Superpower"

"Stinking, rotten crusader"

"There is no...

craziness, imperialism, irresponsibility and irrationality in this world like Reagan."

–United Press International, *January 1, 1986*

"I think we would understand each other if we were together. I can convince him, because I am right and he is wrong. We are against terrorism. He has no proof against us."

–Commenting that he would like to meet Ronald Reagan face to fac
United Press International, April 10, 19

“I never

"Naturally, there are imperialist circles manipulating [President Clinton]. Damn them. They are in the Pentagon, State Department, CIA, National Security Council, and the 400 families of the largest companies. These are the hellish circles manipulating the world in the name of America."

–Interview, *Libyan Television Network, August 29, 1997*

even

"My view on [President] Clinton is clear and evident and the whole world knows it, and he himself knows about it. We don't hate him. We consider him a good man. The poor man has been overwhelmed. He has been besieged or encircled by terrorists (and people who) are very deceptive. But he himself is a good man. But he cannot achieve what he wants."

–Interview, *December 1997*

thought of

"There is no difference between Nazi imperialism and the imperialism led by Ronald Reagan."

–Speech to local political group, *The Associated Press, January 16, 19*

assassinating

"[President Clinton] is really a good man. He is not evil. He is not vindictive. He wants to spenc his days and he wants to get out of the White House and his problems would be finished... We have no history with him, as was the case with Reagan who killed our children and hated me personally. He was mad. Thank God he is suffering from the worst diseases now. God is tormenting him in his life."

—Interview, *Libyan Television Network, August 29, 1*

Reagan."

—Newsweek, *February 22, 1988*

THE SEXES

"If human society reached the stage where man existed without a family, it would become a society of tramps, without roots, like artificial plants."

–The Green Book, *Part 3, Chapter 2*

"I encourage women to be free. I feel women everywhere are oppressed and I would like to see a world of men and women equal."

–The Associated Press, *January 13, 1986*

"There must be a world revolution which puts an end to all materialistic conditions hindering woman from performing her natural role in life and driving her to carry out man's duties in order to be equal in rights…If a woman carries out man's work, she will be transformed into a man abandoning her role."

–The Green Book, *Part 3, Chapter 5*

"The woman, who nature has assigned a natural role different from that of man, must be in an appropriate position to perform her natural role. Motherhood is the female's function, not the male's. Consequently, it is unnatural to separate children from their mother. Any attempt to take children away from their mother is coercion, oppression and dictatorship. The mother who abandons her maternity contradicts her natural role in life. She must be provided with her rights and conditions which are appropriate, non-coercive and unoppressive. Thus she can carry out her natural role under natural conditions."

–The Green Book, *Part 3, Chapter 5*

"Societies in which the existence and unity of the family are threatened, in any circumstances, are similar to fields whose plants are in danger of being swept away or threatened by drought or fire, or of withering away. The blossoming garden or field is that whose plants grow, blossom, pollinate and root naturally. The same holds true for human society."

–The Green Book, *Part 3, Chapter 2*

"On Judgment Day, God does not differentiate between male and female, man and woman. Allah looks upon us as human beings, mankind. Allah sees our deeds. He does not look to our complexion, to our clothes."

–Interview, *December 1997*

"The Islamic woman should be

strong.

She should be trained so that...

she can **defend herself**,
she can **defend her religion**,
she can **defend Islam**."

–Interview, *December 1997*

"All societies nowadays look upon woman

–The Green Book, *Part 3, Chapter 5*

as no more than an article of merchandise. The East regards her as a commodity for buying and selling, while the West does not recognize her femininity."

It is an undisputed fact that both man and woman are human beings. It follows s a self-evident fact that woman and man are equal as human beings.)iscrimination between man and woman is a flagrant act of oppression without ny justification. For woman eats and drinks as man eats and drinks...Woman oves and hates as man loves and hates...Woman feels hunger and thirst as man eels hunger and thirst...Woman lives and dies as man lives and dies."

The Green Book, *Part 3, Chapter 5*

"A tribe is a family which has grown as a result of procreation. It follows that a tribe is a big family. Equally a nation is a tribe which has grown through procreation. The nation, then, is a big tribe. So the world is a nation which has been ramified into various nations. The world, then, is a big nation...However, the degree of warmth involved diminishes as the relationship moves from the smaller level to the larger one."

–The Green Book, *Part 3, Chapter 3*

TER-
RORIS
M

"Libya cannot be patient forever to live under America's international terrorism."

—The Toronto Star, *January 26, 1986*

"We are facing real terrorism this time. This is the worst form of terrorism, physically and psychologically. This weapon is the most vicious form of mass-destruction. It is not restricted to any peculiar time or place. The atom bomb, despite its huge destruction, is far more benign in comparison…I cannot imagine that a human being could use germs against another human being, no matter the degree of hostility was between them. It is in fact a cowardly, satanic and irresponsible use."

–Condemning anthrax attacks in the U.S., *Jamahiriya News Agency, October 20, 2001*

"America has the right to retaliate with direct military action; this is the right of self-defense. [But] we have to sit down... to define what is terrorism, with emotions... otherwise terrorism will win... I'm neither with America nor with terrorism."

–Referring to September 11 terrorist attacks, *interview, Qatari television channel Al-Jazeera, October 24, 2001*

"We are… against terrorism clearly and definitely."

–Chicago Tribune, *April 28, 1986*

"Everyone should put human considerations above political differences… and offer aid to the victims of this gruesome act."

–On victims of the September 11, 2001 terrorist attacks in the U.S., *Boston Herald, Wednesday, September 12, 2001*

—The Associated Press, *January 10, 1986*

"If [Libyan politician] Abu Nidal is a terrorist and [PLO leader] Yasser Arafat is a terrorist and M Khadafy is a terrorist, then George Washington was a terrorist, Lincoln was a **terrorist.**"

PER-SONAL BOMBING RAID (APRIL 15, 1986)

"The greatest thrill of my **life.**"

–British airman, on the bombing raid that killed Khadafy's daughter and wounded his two sons, *Chicago Tribune, April 28, 1986*

“Violence cannot be finished by an air raid on Lybia or on my tent, and this raid on my tent will not finish the struggle for freedom.”

–Chicago Tribune, *April 28, 1986*

"[The house] came down like a heap of rubble.

–On the U.S.-led bombing raid that killed his adopted daughter and wounded two of his sons, *Chicago Tribune, April 28, 1986*

I started to save the children. It wa difficult, groping my way between the bombs and the ashes."

"Reagan's government should collapse, and he should be put on trial as a war criminal and murderer of children. Reagan has issued orders to his armed forces to kill our children. We have not issued any orders to murder anybody...We will not kill your children. We are not like you."

–The Associated Press, *April 17, 1986*

"There was disappointment among the guys that Khadafy survived. The first question I asked was, 'Did we get him?'"

–British airman who did not fly in the bombing raid, *Chicago Tribune, April 28, 1986*

"Khadafy would have to hire every Madison Avenue PR firm to get what Reagan is providing him with."

–French official, *referring to bombing raid, Newsweek, April 21, 1986*

"Reagan has successfully made Khadafy the hero of the Third World."

—Former Austrian Chancellor Bruno Kreisky, referring to the "senseless" U.S.-led air strike on Libya, *United Press International, April 29, 1986*

"We hoped we would get him, but nobody was sure where he would be that night."

–Unnamed U.S. official, on the bombing raid, who added that the National Security Council had prepared a statement calling Khadafy's death "fortuitous." *Maclean's, April 28, 1986*

"Ironically,

he is surviving now largely because of the escalating American campaign against him, which has rallied patriotic Libyans to support a regime they otherwise dislike."

–Lisa Anderson, political science professor, *Columbia University, Maclean's, April 28, 1986*

"We weren't out to

kill

anybody."

–President Ronald Reagan, *denying that Khadafy was a specific target, The Associated Press, April 17, 1986*

HIM-
SELF

"I work 25 hours a day

—but reading is part of the work, and I am a slow reader. Often I have to read things several times to understand."

–National Geographic, *November 1, 2000*

"I see the press as being the messengers between me and the world to tell them the truth."

–Interview, *Daily Mail, March 1986*

"[Some people] have tried to **liquidate me** [but] none of them have come near me—yet."

–Newsweek, *February 22, 1988*

"Bedouin society made me discover the natural laws, natural relationships, life in its true nature and what suffering was like before life knew oppression and exploitation…It gave me a chance which has never been given to anybody else in my position. I have known and lived life in its very primitive stages. Because of that early life, a very simple life, I have lived life in its various stages right up to this modern age of imperialism when life became very complicated, very abnormal and unnatural…I had a general idea how to make the masses free, how to make man happy. After that, things started to get clearer."

–Interview, *New Africa, February 1983*

"Look at them. They are all wearing vests. That's because I wore a vest yesterday. Whenever I wear something, the whole country winds up wearing it."

–Commenting on attendees to Libyan people's assembly, *interview, The New York Times, June 14, 1986*

"It was difficult in terms of th
under which I lived. Bedouin life
therefore comes from the severity
free. We were Bedouins enjoying fu
and everything was absolutely pure, in i
land and there was nothing between

"[Americans] think I don't laugh or smile or tell jokes. They think I only hate."

–Interview, *The New York Times, June 14, 1986*

rcumstances and the environment obile; the strictness of upbringing ese circumstances. But socially I was eedom and we lived amongst nature ue self, in front of us. We lived on the d the sky."

–On his childhood, *in Mirella Bianco, Gadafi: Voice from the Desert (1975)*

AFRICA

“I helped [Nelson] Mandela for a long time, I helped [Yoweri] Museveni [of Uganda] by air-dropping weapons to him close to Kampala, I helped [Robert] Mugabe [of Zimbabwe], I helped Sam Nujoma [of Namibia], I helped [Joachim] Chissano of Mozambique. All these people I helped now travel around the world as heads of state and are kissed by the same people who call me a terrorist!”

–Referring to African leaders he has assisted,
The Independent, March 22, 2000

"Who made the AIDS virus? Some say it's from monkeys in Africa. Those monkeys have been here for centuries. How can it appear now? [Drug companies] seem to even enjoy our suffering. They want to earn billions. Maybe they have a vaccine. They could have discovered it only yesterday. OK. You can get a vaccine now. This is right. The drug companies want to hold it back. It allows them more time to make more and more dollars [CIA agents] manufactured things in their labs and created the AIDS virus. They have tried this on the Haiti people, who were just used as experimental subjects."

–Speech at African AIDS summit meeting, *The Boston Globe, April 29, 2001*

"The [African] liberation battle is not finished yet until all whites leave. When they leave, they must leave the land and all the property because this is our property and they took it by force. What was taken by force you should get by force."

—At dinner hosted by Zimbabwean President Robert Mugabe, *Africa News*, July 30, 2001

MIS-CELLAN EOUS

"No doubt the Arabs need to be provoked, because currently they lack seriousness. They want to die without a cost, without resistance. They are offering themselves on a plate to the worthless enemy. If a summit with [Israel] or America was called, they would have met immediately, but when an Arab summit is called they do not respond."

–On his hopes for Arab unity, *Libyan Television Network, August 29, 1997*

"It is not like writing an ordinary book. It was simply an attempt to explain the dialectic which exists between Marxism and capitalism. The world has reached a political and economic impasse, and humanity simply cannot accept this impasse and accept to die. There must be a way out. That way out is this new theory."

–On writing The Green Book, *New Africa, February 1983*

"George Washington...Abraham Lincoln...Egypt's late Gamal Abdul Nasser, India's Mahatma Gandhi, Sun Yat-Sen of China and Italy's Garibaldi and Mazzini."

–On which world leaders he admires, *interview with Western journalists, January 1986*

"We have just finished making military plans for confrontation in response to the latest American threats against us. So far we have not instructed such actions, such attacks. [But] it is axiomatic that if aggression is staged against us, then we shall escalate the violence, civilian and non-civilian, throughout the world."

–After meeting with Libyan military commanders, *The Associated Press, April 10, 1986*

"We want to mobilize the millions of Muslims from the start of this year to show off our power. We want to show Islam's power and its ability to challenge and return the insults to those who voice them...It is not a secret that America and Europe are leading a campaign to insult and belittle the Islamic peoples."

–Speech, *Xinhua News Agency, May 11, 1997*

"We seized power, and then we handed the authority and the power to the people on the second of March 1977. For these reasons, the

Libyan people have no opposition in politics or in authority or in power because they wield power. They are in power."

–Interview, *December 1997*

“The whole world knows...

ıat it was a premeditated murder. The file contains enough evi-
ence for the world."

–On the death of Diana, *Princess of Wales.*

"Libyans can watch

anything they want, but visitors should learn

about Libya."

–On why he does not permit foreign broadcasts in Libyan hotels, *National Geographic, November 1, 2000*

–Denying any Libyan role in the bombing of Pan Am

"[The Lockerbie bombing case] only represents part of a series of confrontations between the oppressed and the oppressors, freedom fighters and imperialists, angels and devils, and good and evil."

Flight 103 over Lockerbie, Scotland, *Deutsche Presse-Agentur, February 5, 2001*

"We are not concerned with the

Middle East.

We are not in the

Middle East."

–Interview, *Libyan Television Network, August 29, 1997*

"We are a backward country.

People don't understand

that we are damaging the land,

damaging the environment."

–National Geographic, *November 1, 2000*

"Crush stray dogs like cats."

–Instructions to Libyans abroad to assassinate Libyan critics who have sought sanctuary abroad, *The New York Times, June 14, 1986*

OTH-
ERS ON
KHADA
FY

"I am leaving you, I say to you: My brother Moammer Khadafy is the representative of Arab nationalism, of the Arab revolution and Arab unity. My dear brothers, may God watch over you for the well being of the Arab people. May you go from victory to victory, for your victories are the victories of the Arab people."

–Gamal Abdul Nasser, *Egyptian father of Arab nationalism, shortly before his death, at a rally at Benghazi*

"Khadafy is an anomaly. He stands out as a sore thumb who keeps taunting the world. Nothing seems to stop him."

–State Department official. *The Boston Globe, January 5, 1989*

"It is in the desert that one must seek out the very essence of Khadafy's nature, of the spirituality, of the mysticism which have greater weight than any of his aspirations, and which influence even his political action...It is precisely this concept of liberty, the intangible freedom of desert people—a freedom entirely one's own and yet a submission to God, and God alone—which underlies all the choices, decisions and actions taken by Khadafy; even, and perhaps essentially, those of a political nature. To his way of thinking, there is no salvation for mankind or for the nations unless they believe in God and cling to those moral values which no coercion can enforce, and which can arise only from faith."

–Mirella Bianco, *Gadafi: Voice from the Desert (1975)*

"Here we are, just a nation of 3 million desert people, and the whole world is watching us. This could not be without Khadafy."

–Libyan man, *The Courier-Journal, January 19, 1989*

"It was hard to credit that this was the man President Reagan had condemned as the world's number one terrorist. Colonel Moammar Khadafy was simple and charming sitting by the bonfire outside his tent when I arrived to interview him."

–Daily Mail, *March 1986*

"Man of faith and tradition, Moammar Khadafy cannot be classified according to the criteria commonly admitted. If you search for him on the right you will find him on the left, since he preaches in many ways a renovation with the air of revolution. But if you look for him on the left you risk finding him on the right, because this sincere mystic is tied to more than one traditional value. It is not Khadafy who is senseless; it is the terms, obsolete, and upon which are based the subjective judgments of foreign observers who are more interested in polemic than in the truth."

–Professor Francis Dessart, Chairman, *U.N. Commission on Human Rights and Religious Freedom*

"For the first time, an Arab politician has transformed himself into an outstanding writer with his own distinguished style, derived from his vision of the Arab reality. Khadafy wanted to send warning messages through the set of stories, and raise a cry against drowning ourselves in a sea of pollution, subjugations, myths and illusions, all in a smooth, lavish style."

–Iqbal Baraka, editor of Hawaa magazine, on the publication of Khadafy's children's book *The Village Is the Village, the Land Is the Land, and the Suicide of the Spaceman, which sold 100,000 copies in its first two weeks, United Press International March 15, 1996*

"He has become like Yasir Arafat, constantly in motion and terrified of being killed."

–Arab diplomat, *The New York Times, June 14, 1986*

"I don't want Khadafy anywhere in the United States. And being a Californian, that's the last place I'd send him."

–Ronald Reagan, *challenging the accuracy of the San Francisco/AIDS exchange, The Record (Bergen), October 3, 1986*

"Why not invite Khadafy to San Francisco; he likes to dress up so much."

–Ronald Reagan, *The Record (Bergen), October 3, 1986*

"I consider this a bit of a joke."

–Gaber Khadafyarmouti, arts writer for al-Hayat newspaper, *on the publication of Khadafy's children's book The Village Is the Village, the Land Is the Land, and the Suicide of the Spaceman, United Press International, March 15, 1996*

"If Kirkegaard was right, and purity of heart is to will one thing and one thing only, then Khadafy was the purest-hearted military conspirator ever to seize control of a nation. He did not drink or smoke, there are no tales of youthful passion; he appeared to have no personal life at all."

–T.D. Allman, *Vanity Fair*

"I just think that the man is a zealot. He's pursuing a revolutionary cause that could affect a great many countries."

–Ronald Reagan, *press conference, November 1985*

"Why don't we give him AIDS!"

–Secretary of State George Schultz's alleged response, *The Record (Bergen), October 3, 1986*

"The popularity and success of Khadafy, over the period of the 1970s, was based overwhelmingly on the fact that the country was so rich that he was able to export revolution and pay for these foreign adventures, but at the same time was able to guarantee a good high standard of living at home, a great change over the monarchy before the revolution. [But now] the system is fundamentally in jeopardy."

–Michael Collins Dunn, *Georgetown University Center for Contemporary Arab Studies, The Toronto Star, April 18, 1986*

"The idea that Khadafy can press a button and there is a terrorist act is ridiculous. Khadafy will always be a friend of any radical. But he is only one among many others to support these [Palestinian terrorist] groups."

–Bruno Kreisky, *former Austrian chancellor, United Press International, May 5, 1986*

"With Minister Farrakhan's vision and Colonel Khadafy's resources, African-Americans should be able to establish an independent political party that breaks the hegemony to two political parties in this country...the Demopublicans and the Republicrats."

–Brooklyn Attorney Colin Moore, *on Khadafy's pledge of one billion dollars to help blacks in America "get their political act together," New York Amsterdam News, February 3, 1996*

"Khadafy was deeply distressed."

–Libyan source, *on reports that Khadafy's life was saved during an assassination attempt by a female bodyguard who took rebel bullets herself and died instantly, The Mirror, June 12, 1998*

"He is judged to suffer from a severe personality disturbance—a "borderline personality disorder"...under severe stress he is subject to episodes of bizarre behavior when his judgment may be faulty."

–Classified CIA profile of Khadafy, *1982*

"If a coup takes place, that's all to the good. There are lots of people in Libya who think that Libya would be better off if Khadafy weren't there. And there are even more people outside of Libya who think that."

–U.S. Secretary of State George Schultz, *Chicago Tribune, April 19, 1986*

"Everyone's entitled to call him whatever animal they want, but I think he's more than a bad smell."

–President Ronald Reagan, *on former President Jimmy Carter's criticism that U.S. policy toward Khadafy should not be to "poke a polecat," The Associated Press, April 10, 1986*

$1,770 for planting a bomb

$5,330 for a submachine gun attack

$53,330 (in advance) for planning and carrying out a suicide attack

–Khadafy's "price list" of payments for various terrorist attacks, *based on Israeli and Lebanese intelligence reports, Chicago Tribune, April 20, 1986*

"If only the U.S. would leave Khadafy alone, he would just fade away into nothing, but this just feeds his ego and encourages him…The situation also helps Khadafy's image because it makes what he has been saying about imperialists conspiring against him seem true."

–Arab diplomat, *The New York Times, March 28, 1986*

"If the man would conduct himself within the norms of international behavior, he could run his country. But when he starts exporting terrorism, then that's when he needs to be put back in his box."

–Larry Speakes, *Ronald Reagan's press spokesman, Chicago Tribune, March 26, 1986*

"Khadafy is his own smoking gun."

–U.S. Secretary of State George Shultz, *responding to threats against Israel and the United States during a speech by Khadafy, The Washington Post, January 17, 1986*

"I'm baffled by the motives of the Americans, unless they want an excuse to just blow him up. It would be much better to ignore him, which infuriates him. This has gotten him the kind of support he could not have engendered himself."

–Western diplomat, *The New York Times, March 28, 1986*

"It's political exploitation of both sides, I think. Khadafy proved he can fight when the death line, as he called it, was crossed. And the Americans proved they could cross. So they must both be very happy."

–Western diplomat, *The New York Times, March 28, 1986*

"I'm going to the Bab al-Azzizya to kill Khadafy. I'm sure they will kill me, but when you hear that Khadafy is dead, move your troops from Siirt to Tripoli."

–Col. Khassan Ishqal, *Khadafy's cousin and fellow tribesman and governor of Siirt province, before attempting to assassinate Khadafy with a machine gun and dying in the attempt, United Press International, January 14, 1986*

"I doubt very much that the American people, if they knew, would want to subsidize Khadafy's terrorism, yet that is what they're being forced to do."

–U.S. Rep. David R. Obey, *Chairman of the House Appropriations Subcommittee on Foreign Operations, on the fact that five American oil companies continued to distribute and market a significant share of Libyan oil despite the deteriorating diplomatic situation, The Washington Post, April 24, 1986*

"No course of action short of stimulating Khadafy's fall will bring any significant and enduring change in Libyan policies."

–Secret CIA plan to topple Khadafy's regime, *leaked to press, United Press International, November 3, 1985*

"A judicious political calculator."

–Profile of Khadafy in secret CIA plan to topple his regime, *leaked to press, United Press International, November 3, 1985*

"To [Khadafy], the symbol he exports to his people is more important than the reality of his action."

–Western ambassador, *Tripoli, The Associated Press, January 26, 1986*

"The last thing we want is to get into a shooting match with Khadafy. The plan is psywar: keep the pressure up, keep Khadafy on the boil."

–U.S. State Department official, *on U.S. "naval exercise" in the Mediterranean, Newsweek, February 3, 1986*

"It wasn't an unusual thing we set out to do. He opened the hostilities. We closed them."

–President Ronald Reagan, *on U.S. bombing raids on Libya, United Press International, April 9, 1986*

"The outside world thinks that this country consists of a man and a desert. But we are more than that."

–Mohammed al-Allasi, *Libyan playwright, National Geographic, November 1, 2000.*

"He's obviously a coward. He didn't put himself in a vulnerable position. He wants to live. He didn't think we'd come after him."

–U.S. State Department Official, *on Khadafy's reaction to U.S. bombing raids, United Press International, April 18, 1986*